Praise for *Communi*

Rich, Dense, Practical—

L. Bonita Patterson's newest book is filled with valuable worksheets, tools and thought-provoking ideas to encourage the reader to immerse in the Communication Under Fire (CUF) process. The worksheets are particularly useful. They are constructed so you dig deeply into your own communication process to explore how your feelings often dictate what you say. CUF is an active, engaging book that is sure to make a difference to the reader who works it through. I highly recommend it!

> Charlotte S. Waisman, Ph.D.
> *Principal, The AthenA Group*

L. Bonita Patterson's *Communication Under Fire* is a great way to enhance the communication process in your organization or family. The tips are "right on" and the worksheets help give you the insight you need to communicate when it is most critical. As a CEO I highly recommend everyone experience *Communication Under Fire,* you'll be glad you did.

> Jim Burr, SPHR CFI
> *President/CEO*
> *Western Air Enterprises*

Communication Under Fire is refreshing, insightful, and a **must** for personal and professional growth. It shares the tools and principles that will enhance your leadership skills make a difference in your life.

This book has given me a new way of analyzing effective communication. It held my interest and left me excited about using new skills and techniques to communicate more effectively with coworkers, friends, and family.

> Denise Meekins McBride
> *First Vice President,*
> *Community Economic Development*
> *SunTrust Bank*

L. Bonita Patterson is one of those rare individuals who put into practice her beliefs and she has poured out her long-standing, yet proven, knowledge in the pages of this manual. She shares her unique approach to challenging communications and has organized it into a practical, step-by-step format that you can use right away. It is "must have" for every individual who wants to improve their relationships — whether at work or at home.

> Karen Armon, *Founder and Creator of the MarketOne Executive*™.

The problem I have had with books about improving my communications is that they have, at least for me, usually failed to communicate clearly how to do so. They have been heavy on theory and light on practice. L. Bonita Patterson's *Communication Under Fire* describes clearly and concisely how one might go about communicating more effectively when things might easily go awry. She draws upon the work of Goleman and others while providing her own unique flavor, which is obviously grounded in her observations and experience helping others to become more effective communicators.

Bonita provides a model of communications styles and asks us to look at ourselves while we develop a better understanding of the communications styles of those we live and work with. She helps us understand why we communicate as ineffectively as we often do, while our intention is just the opposite, describes the early warning signals of an impending communications disaster, and provides practical tools to improve our effectiveness.

The exercises and worksheets make reading *Communication Under Fire* more like a classroom experience than a text, increasing the likelihood that some of the material will actually influence our communications skills and abilities. I recommend L. Bonita Patterson's new book as a valuable addition to the literature on communicating more effectively.

> Kenneth J. Lamport
> *Human Resource Business Partner*
> *Seagate Technology*

Communication Under Fire presents challenging concepts in an understandable and easy-to-read style. The intuitive activities will help readers become aware of their hot buttons and alarms, to know how to communicate effectively in challenging situations. These tools can be applied both at work and at home to help build strong relationships.

> Christine E Homer, SPHR
> *Sr. Director, Organization Development*
> *Time Warner Cable*

Communication Under Fire gets to the heart of communicating effectively. The streamlined format delivers information and tools in a concise and compelling way that makes it easy to read and put to use. It prepares you to handle CUF (tough) conversations successfully.

> Kim Sharp
> *Vice President, Diversity*
> *HCA*

Communication Under Fire™

How To Talk When Things Heat Up

L. Bonita Patterson
President
Polaris Consulting Group
303.634.4253
bonita@polarisconsulting.biz
www.polarisconsulting.biz

AuthorHouse™
1663 Liberty Drive, Suite 200
Bloomington, IN 47403
www.authorhouse.com
Phone: 1-800-839-8640

First published by AuthorHouse 5/4/2007

ISBN: 978-1-4343-0368-4

Printed in the United States of America
Bloomington, Indiana

This book is printed on acid-free paper.

Dedication

This book is dedicated to my parents, Chick & Bunny, who are the greatest treasures of my life. All of my accomplishments have been built on the foundation of their loving hearts.

In my most trying times, if I rely on the communication principles and tools in this book, I hope I can display some of the strength, grace, and understanding that have always been their example to me.

Communication Under Fire

Acknowledgements

I thank my dear friends and colleagues for their support, enthusiasm, and belief in the power of positive intention.

Christine Homer, Karen Armon, Anna Huff, and Kathleen Winsor-Games who where there at the genesis of this concept. Their encouragement helped me understand the importance of sharing this information with others.

Richie Fontenot Hunter, who ignited the spark of urgency to complete this project.

Earl Suttle, whose mentoring has been invaluable.

Jake Adam York, whose flair and talent for language made him the perfect editor.

A special thanks to Nancy Bellony, whose tireless attention to detail and insightful comments helped streamline this powerful message.

Communication Under Fire

Table of Contents

Introduction

Purpose

In most areas of life, effective communication enhances success. Whether in the business world or in our personal lives, we must interact and share information with others. When things are calm and the risks are low, most of us do a good job, but when the heat is turned up, it becomes more difficult to have a productive conversation. This manual addresses the dynamics of high-intensity conversations and the challenges they present, and teaches you to overcome those challenges and become a more effective communicator.

Audience

This manual is designed for individuals seeking to improve their communication effectiveness. Conceptual information provides insight into the communication process to help you understand the factors involved in successful conversation.

The activities and worksheets help you apply the principles, tools, and techniques to your situation. These activities help you tailor the system to your particular needs so you may benefit more quickly.

How To Use This Manual

The best way to leverage the information in this manual is to identify your difficult communication situations — past, present, and future — and keep them in mind as you work through the material. Constantly ask yourself how you could apply the information discussed in the manual to improve your effectiveness in those situations. Thus you compel yourself to stretch beyond your comfort zone to apply the tools and principles to help improve those situations.

There are opportunities for you to engage in activities to help anchor a skill or concept, make commitments to take you beyond this manual, and help you implement the skills and practices in your daily life. The following alert you to those opportunities:

- Activity

- Activity Worksheet

- Commitment

- Quote

Terminology

The term CUF (Communication Under Fire) is used in the following manner:
- To describe the Communication Under Fire™ System
- To indicate a tough, heated, or high-intensity conversation or situation

Chapter 1
Overview

Impact of Communication

Humans have been communicating for tens of thousands of years. You'd think we'd be experts by now. Well, we are experts — experts in our own style, however effective or ineffective it is.

Communication is a complex, multi-dimensional process. It is a critical aspect of building trust and deepening relationships. It involves our words, expressions, body language, tone, volume, and emotions. Our constant challenge is to calibrate all of these elements to optimize results.

How we communicate reflects how we feel about:
- Ourselves
- Our environment
- Other people
- What is happening, or not, in our lives

The trick is to hit the right note in our communication even when it is difficult. This manual focuses on how to communicate effectively in heated situations.

Communication has a dramatic impact on the bottom line of any business. According to The Public Relations Society of America (2003), The Institute of Healthcare Advancement (Symanovich, 2003), and The Gartner Group (Gallagher, 2001), organizations are impacted in the following ways (see next page):

Industry	Impact
General Business	Companies who communicated in a straightforward, effective manner had 85% more net earnings than those who focused on "spin" and "jargon"
Healthcare	Lose $7.3 billion annually due to miscommunication among health care professionals and with the consumer
Technology	80% of the reason for project failure is due to poor communication between business and technology managers

In the following areas, how would your **organization** improve if people communicated more effectively?

Morale

_____

_____

_____

_____

Productivity

_____

_____

_____

_____

Customer Service

_____

_____

_____

_____

Organization / Business Results

_____

_____

_____

_____

Other

_____

_____

_____

_____

_____

_____

_____

_____

Which of these areas (morale, productivity, customer service, organization / business results, other) impacts you the most? Why?

Communication is the key to all healthy relationships. The success or failure of a marriage is determined by the effectiveness of communication, as is the openness and mutuality of relationships between parents and children.

 In the following areas, how would your **personal** life improve by communicating more effectively?

Attitude

_____

_____

_____

_____

Happiness/Optimism

_____

_____

_____

_____

Self-Regard

_____

_____

_____

_____

Confidence

_____

_____

_____

_____

Other

_____

_____

_____

_____

_____

Communication Process

Let us look at two views of the communication process — the Standard Communication Process, which identifies the mechanics of the interchange, and the Communication Under Fire™ Process, which focuses on the behaviors necessary to effectively navigate turbulent situations.

Standard Process

The Standard Communication Process begins when the sender has a thought or idea to convey. The sender then communicates the message via a specific channel or medium. The sender receives the information and decides what it means and how he or she feels about it. Then the receiver sends a message back.

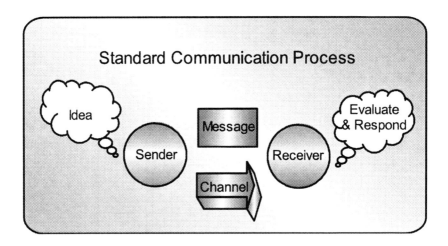

The key insight is that the receiver hears something, and then evaluates what was heard according to his or her own filters. The receiver's values, experiences, and expectations can filter out or amplify certain messages, which can result in the receiver hearing something very different than what the sender intended. Two examples of this are:

1. A manager telling an employee that if he or she exceeds expectations then a promotion might be considered. The employee hears, "I will get a promotion if I exceed objectives."
   - How might the employee react if he or she exceeds expectations and does not get promoted?
   - If the employee reacts negatively, how might the manager respond to keep the lines of communication open?
   - If this is not resolved, and two-way communication is not reestablished, could it diminish their trust level?
2. I told my young cousin that if my schedule permitted, she could visit me in Colorado for two weeks in the summer. She was so excited that she heard me say she could **definitely** come visit in the summer.
   - How might she react if I am traveling too much for her to visit?
   - Could she view my next "promise" with less enthusiasm?
   - Would it diminish her trust in me?
   - If we do not effectively deal with this, could our relationship suffer?

Communication Under Fire™ *(CUF) Process*

In addition to understanding the Standard Communication Process just discussed, there are additional aspects to consider in tough situations.

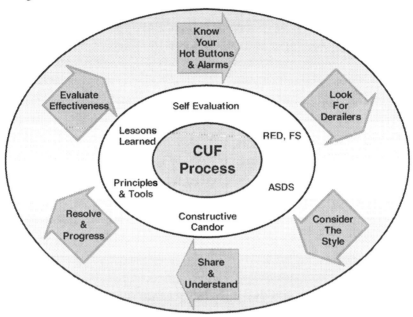

First, know your personal **hot buttons**. Be aware of words, attitudes, expressions, or environments that cause overreaction or shut-down.

Second, look for signs of communication **derailers.** Identify any factors that increase the chances of having a difficult conversation. Then determine what you can do to eliminate or minimize those factors so they do not negatively impact the interaction.

Third, consider the communication style you are using and that of the other person. If you are using an ineffective style, if you are avoiding the issue or dominating the conversation, shift to an approach that will increase your opportunity for success. If the other person is using a difficult style, such as agreeing with you when they really see things differently, you should utilize the CUF principles and tools to achieve the best outcome.

Fourth, share your view of the situation and ask the other person to share their perspective. If the other person is reluctant, you should help them feel more comfortable and better understand the benefits of opening up. When the other person does share their viewpoint, really listen and consider what they say.

Fifth, build on the success of the fourth step to resolve issues impeding your progress and strive to create a solution that addresses the needs and expectations of both parties.

Finally, spend time debriefing the conversation to evaluate your level of success. Write down what went well and what could have been improved, such as the tone and direction of the conversation. Pinpoint any counterproductive behaviors you exhibited and consider how you can avoid them in future conversations.

Each of the above process steps will be addressed in subsequent chapters. Note that 'Know Your Hot Buttons & Alarms' is the first step in the CUF Process, but it is one of the last chapters in the manual, because you will be identifying them as we progress through each topic. In Chapter 7 (Hot Buttons & Alarms) the information is consolidated.

As you can see, the CUF advantage is having a tool that helps improve your professional and personal communication to enhance your success. It addresses the key aspects of effective communication including skills and techniques, emotional factors, and continuous improvement.

Chapter 2
Dimensions & Derailers

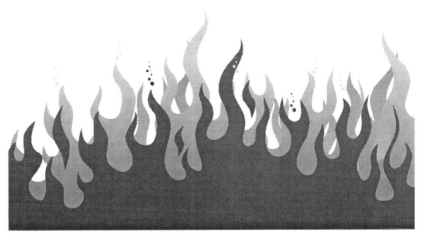

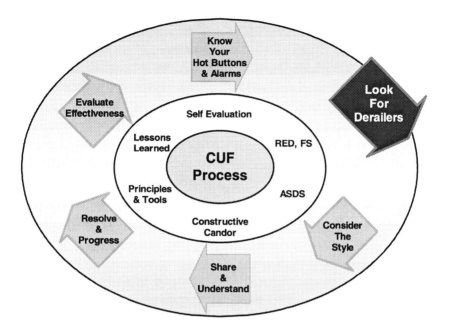

Well-intentioned plans can go awry when dealing with the unexpected. The purpose of this chapter is to explore six factors that can shut down conversations or get them off track. Increased awareness of communication derailers and how to overcome them, strengthens your ability to navigate tough situations.

Risk, Emotions, and Differences (RED)

CUF conversations can be characterized by the presence of risk, emotions, and/or differences. Conversations can derail if those involved perceive:

- Potential risk or threat
- Distracting emotions
- Barriers between themselves and another person

Risk

The first element of RED is Risk, which Merriam-Webster (2006) defines as the, "possibility of loss, injury, disadvantage, or destruction." People do what is necessary to protect themselves from harm. Risk can include the possibility of loss, injury, disadvantage, or destruction to personal, professional, physical, mental (intellectual), and emotional well being.

Personal Risk is the potential for negative impact on quality of personal relationships. For example, under real or perceived threat of losing the house or car someone might adopt an overbearing and destructive communication style that is not conducive to building relationships or to solving problems collaboratively.

Professional Risk is the possibility of losing credibility, stature, access, or clout. You may have witnessed or experienced a situation I have seen happen repeatedly in organizations — someone says something politically incorrect and suddenly others take longer to return that person's phone calls, or they "forget" to invite the person to key meetings. This results in the loss of access to coworkers and information, which leads to being out of the loop — a deadly situation for an ambitious employee.

Physical Risk is the prospect of injury. If you feel physically threatened by someone, are you likely to want to freely share information with them? Probably not.

Mental or Intellectual Risk is the danger of thinking too far outside the box. Much is written about the benefits of creative thinking. There is abundant research on how new ideas and new ways of doing things have helped companies capture market share and increase profit, helped government organizations better serve the public, helped scientists develop cures and treatments for diseases, and helped people creatively finance their homes. However, ingenuity is not always rewarded. Galileo experienced the downside risk of coloring too far outside the lines. His belief in the Copernican Theory that the earth revolves around the sun — not the reverse — put him at risk with the authorities of his time.

Emotional Risk is the chance of getting your feelings hurt professionally or personally. It can manifest in the workplace when employees are asked for loyalty and commitment. Sometimes employees are reluctant because they fear that even if they fully buy-in, they could be demoted or fired.

Emotions

The second aspect of RED is Emotions. They have a persuasive influence on our behavior, and filter the information we receive from others. Our emotions impact what we hear and how we respond — anger, fear, laughter. Each emotion elicits specific chemical or hormonal reactions in the body, which are involuntary and automatic. Often our responses are automatic, but they are not involuntary. We have the ability to choose effective behaviors.

Which column of emotions listed below are more likely to negatively impact communication?

Emotions	
Anger	**Joy**
Fear	**Happiness**
Contempt	**Optimism**
Sorrow	**Acceptance**
Disgust	**Anticipation**
Envy	**Surprise**

The left column. Those emotions release stress-related chemicals, such as the hormone adrenaline, which prepares the body for physical exertion by increasing the heart rate, raising the blood pressure, and releasing sugar stored in the liver for quick energy. Excess adrenaline can lead to aggressive behavior.

The right column produces such chemicals as endorphins, which produce a calm or euphoric feeling often referred to as a natural high.

The emotional brain is responsible for regulating emotion, motivation, smell, aggression, sensuality, and desire. It is also the seat of an automatic phenomenon called the fight-or-flight response. In earlier times, primitive humans routinely faced situations in which they had to stay and fight to the death, or to flee to safety. For most of us, this is no longer the case. However, the stressors of our lives — being cut off in traffic, someone cutting in line, hearing loud cell phone talking, having a colleague scream at you at work, meeting aggressive deadlines — elicit the same chemical reaction in our bodies. We are flooded with adrenaline and other chemicals to fuel us as we fight (get the job done) or take flight (shut down, feel stressed, or miss deadlines).

This is the point at which we have the option of choosing an emotional or a rational response. In the heat of the moment, exercising your options is not easy because it becomes difficult to think. We have all heard the expression, "I was so mad I could not think." The torrent of chemicals produces emotional noise, which interferes with our brains ability to process information. It takes extra effort and commitment to maintain control and respond in an appropriate and effective manner.

A key aspect of this process is that it takes an instant for the chemical flood to occur, but it takes a while for the chemicals to recede to their normal levels. Even though you understand what is happening in your mind and body, and choose to stay in the CUF process, you still have to deal with the chemical excess for a while. There are techniques, such as deep breathing, meditation, biofeedback, and self-talk which can accelerate the return to normalcy.

Emotions can impact our willingness and ability to make effective choices. Knowledge of communication theory, strategies, and techniques will only help you in difficult situations if you strive to consciously override disruptive emotions with rational thought.

Differences

The final element of RED is Differences. We are all unique and can be thrown off balance by individual differences. Most of us appreciate other viewpoints – to a degree. However, differences become problematic when they interfere with our ability to communicate, accomplish objectives, and resolve issues.

Leveraging RED

Use RED as a tool to:
- Anticipate what you might encounter in an upcoming conversation
- Analyze the conversation you are currently experiencing
- Debrief a past discussion

Risk

Describe a risky or threatening situation you encountered at work or in your personal life.

_____

_____

_____

_____

_____

_____

_____

_____

_____

Emotions

How did you think and feel in the above situation? How could you have reacted more appropriately and communicated more effectively?

_____

_____

_____

_____

_____

_____

_____

_____

_____

We think differences are obvious and easy to detect until they surface and block effective communication.

Differences

The characteristics listed below are indicative of individual differences.

Learning Styles	*Weight*
Age	*Thinking Preferences*
IQ	*Height*
Emotional Intelligence	*Values*
Gender	*Culture*
Politics	*Hearing Loss*
Religion	

Unconsciously, these differences can get under skin, creating barriers that make it difficult to communicate effectively. How do you respond in situations where these differences are present: Select and discuss 1 or 2 of the above differences.

_____

_____

_____

_____

_____

_____

_____

_____

_____

_____

_____

_____

_____

_____

_____

_____

_____

_____

Fire Starters

In addition to RED, the following three Fire Starters can further intensify a conversation and add fuel to an already raging inferno:

- Pre-emptive Jumps
- Undiscussables
- Left-Hand Column

They address a broad range of issues. Pre-emptive Jumps deals with jumping to conclusions; Undiscussables talks about the hidden issues that constrict conversation, and Left-Hand Column is the place you stuff the things you dare not speak.

Pre-Emptive Jumps

When we get new information we compare it to what we already know and attempt to classify it with our preexisting knowledge. This automatic process happens in an instant and with little conscious thought. However, sometimes we jump to the wrong conclusion and need to challenge ourselves to consciously think situations through.

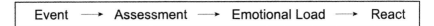

Event ⟶ Assessment ⟶ Emotional Load ⟶ React

The process begins when an event occurs, or something is said or done. We make assumptions about what we see or hear, and draw conclusions about its meaning. The value we place on our interpretation of the event sparks an emotional response. It is from this point of emotional load that we react to the event. Our assessment may be inaccurate, thereby rendering our emotional response and subsequent reaction unsuitable. At this point communication is less than effective. If you are not getting the results you want, reevaluate your interpretation and response, and ask for clarification. In some cases you will get information that will cause you to respond differently.

Undiscussables

Argyris (1990) explored the concept of undiscussables, which are issues that everyone pretends to ignore, and no one discusses.

The purpose of undiscussables is to protect us from embarrassment, harm, and threat. A classic example is the star salesman with the rude and obnoxious demeanor. The star closes the big deals that bring in substantial amounts of revenue and prestige. The other side of the coin is that the star communicates with co-workers by yelling, screaming, and belittling. Management ignores the behavior because they do not want to upset or lose their "cash cow".

Employees know this topic is not open to discussion, and the expectation is to "grin and bear it." The reality is that the yelling behavior negatively impacts the employees. Management's talk about respect and valuing people are viewed by the employees as completely hollow. Morale is bad, relationships are damaged and communication is stifled. Learning and growth are inhibited because the environment is not conducive to information sharing that fosters productivity. There are many reasons for undiscussables, chief among them are fear of reprisal and not wanting to deal with tough issues.

There are three aspects of undiscussables:
1. The problem is ignored
2. Those in power will not directly discuss the issue and how to resolve it
3. The fact that the issue even exists cannot be discussed

The existence of undiscussables reinforces professional and personal dysfunction, and limits open, two-way communication.

Paul Harvey, the radio personality, reported that this was found on a company employee reader board:
"There are only two things you need in life
WD40 to make things go
Duct Tape to make them stop"

More of the Good

In what areas does your team or organization need WD40 (what good things should they **start** doing, or do **more of**)?

_____

_____

_____

_____

_____

_____

_____

What conversations can you have to help get things started?

Person(s)	*Topic*
_____	_____
_____	_____
_____	_____
_____	_____
_____	_____

Do any of these conversations involve undiscussables? If so, what would it take for you to address them?

_____

_____

_____

_____

_____

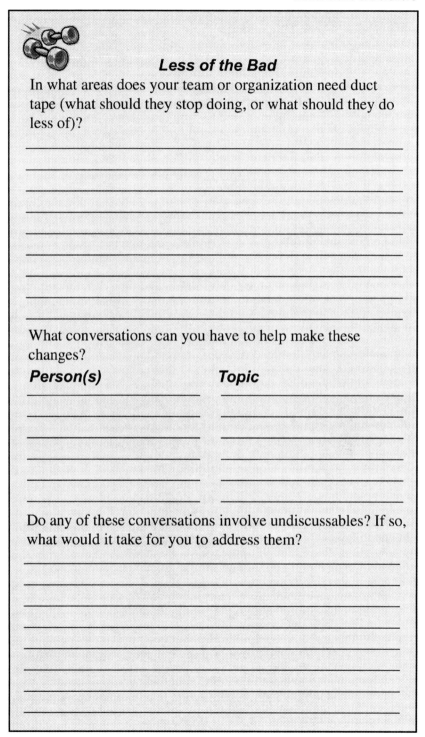

Less of the Bad

In what areas does your team or organization need duct tape (what should they stop doing, or what should they do less of)?

_____

_____

_____

_____

_____

_____

_____

What conversations can you have to help make these changes?

Person(s)	*Topic*
_____	_____
_____	_____
_____	_____
_____	_____
_____	_____

Do any of these conversations involve undiscussables? If so, what would it take for you to address them?

_____

_____

_____

_____

_____

_____

_____

Left-Hand Column

Left-Hand Column is a technique used by Argyris (1990) to help uncover unproductive behaviors in organizations. A group of leaders was asked to write about an organizational problem and instructed to split a page into two columns. On the right-hand side was written, in chronological sequence, what was said in a company meeting by the various participants. On the left-hand column was written real thoughts and feelings that were not communicated.

What was discovered is that the information in the left-hand column was very powerful and that it influenced the communication process. Even when we do not verbalize what is in our left-hand column, it comes out in our tone of voice, body language, or our willingness to engage in **Constructive Candor** with others. When our left-hand columns are full, other people can sense something is going on, even if they do not know exactly what it is.

The left-hand column contains issues you feel and do not verbalize. They remain unresolved and left to fester and become a garbage dump. You do not want to live next door to a garbage dump, so why create a toxic heap in your body?

In the Emotions section of Risk, Emotions, Differences (RED) we discussed two columns of emotions. The emotions on the left side are the ones that reside in your left-hand column — negative and often unspoken.

Emotions	
Anger	*Joy*
Fear	*Happiness*
Contempt	*Optimism*
Sorrow	*Acceptance*
Disgust	*Anticipation*
Envy	*Surprise*

Undiscussables create left-hand column content. These negative emotions that are stuffed in your left-hand column cause hormonal surges that harm your body. If you have garbage in your left-hand column you should focus on constructively clearing it out. For most of us it is an ongoing process — as soon as you clear it out something new happens that creates more emotional sludge.

The impact of having things build up in your left-hand column is that you are missing opportunities to improve conversations, deepen relationships, and get better results.

Think about a frustrating conversation you have had recently, or anticipate having. Using the right side of the page, write down what each of you said. On the left side write down what you were thinking or feeling at each point in the conversation. Do you have unresolved issues in your left-hand column?

Revisit this page after we have discussed how to clear out your left-hand column with the FACT tool in the Chapter 5 (*Resolve & Progress*).

Left Hand Column	*Right Hand Column*

Adapted from Chris Argyris (1990)

Dimensions & Derailers
Hot Buttons & Alarms

Hot buttons are words, issues, attitudes, or situations that cause an immediate negative reaction. What are your hot buttons?

_____

_____

_____

_____

_____

_____

_____

_____

The body sends signals that we are having a negative response. Heavy breathing, shallow breathing, flushing, blinking, staring, chest tightening pacing, and fist pounding are examples of "hot button" signals.

_____

_____

_____

_____

_____

_____

_____

_____

_____

* The Hot Button & Alarms lists at the end of Chapters 2, 3, 4, and 5 will be consolidated in Chapter 7 (*Hot Buttons & Alarms*)

CUF Commitment #1

I will:
- Pay attention to my alarms
- Pause and consider how I am feeling
- Consciously override

☐ I commit

Signature   Date

_____   _____

Chapter 3
CUF Styles

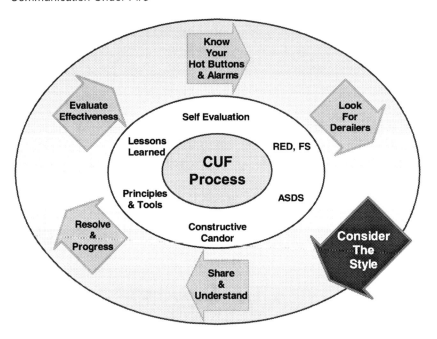

The last chapter explored six derailers that can get a conversation off track. The focus now shifts to the four styles we use when communicating with others. Three of the styles — Avoid, Surrender, and Dominate — are not recommended because they can cause a breakdown in communication. The recommend style — Synergize — can help you move the conversation forward and drive toward a positive outcome.

Style Matrix

In the CUF Styles matrix below, style is determined by the degree to which you focus on accomplishing your objectives (X axis), and the degree to which you collaborate with others in accomplishing their objectives (Y axis). The four Communication Under Fire™ styles are Avoid, Surrender, Dominate, and Synergize.

As we examine the behaviors of each style, identify which behaviors you exhibit and which are exhibited by those with whom you work or live.

CUF Styles

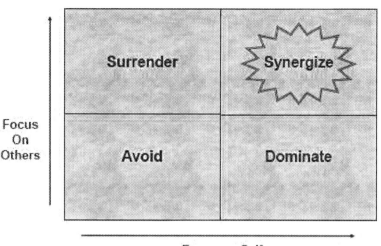

Avoid

Motto — *I'm not dealing with that today*

The Avoid style demonstrates little interest in accomplishing one's own goals or those of other people. The two types of Avoid behaviors are that of the Hider and that of the Dismisser. While they both avoid discussing issues and sharing information, they go about it in very different ways.

Hiders are veiled, disingenuous, and deceptive. Hiders go to great lengths to convince you they are being completely open and honest with you, and freely sharing all information. Their objective is to look earnest, sincere, and completely "on board," but they do not really help or support you. The pitfall in dealing with Hiders is that they use excuses to mislead you into believing they are truly providing valid data, insight, or assistance from them, when you are not. You may observe them delaying, stalling, missing appointments, or interacting only via email or voicemail.

45

Dismissers are obvious, contemptuous, and disdainful. They let you know they are not going to deal with you. They straightforwardly tell you or use body language to convey their message. Dismissers are more aggressive and hostile than Hiders in letting you know where they stand.

The Avoid style is detrimental to good communication, to building relationships, to resolving issues and to creating solutions. When you feel tempted to use this style, challenge yourself to share honestly and receive information that could benefit all participants.

Surrender

Motto — *Sure, whatever you say*

The Surrender style demonstrates little interest in accomplishing one's own goals and a high degree of interest in supporting others in reaching their objectives. The two types of Surrender behavior are that of the **Appeaser** and that of the **Martyr**. Both types will "give it up" to someone else, but one of the styles requires that you acknowledge their sacrifice.

Appeasers are overly amiable, accommodating, and conciliatory. Clearly, we are not talking about people who are friendly and take responsibility for their own objectives. Appeasers abdicate that responsibility. They are totally compliant and want to make others happy, and are not interested in making waves or saying unpopular things. Appeasers are yes men. Appeasers are pleasant, yet frustrating because they will not offer alternatives. Their typical approach is to say what they think you want to hear.

Martyrs are whiners and long-suffering victims. They set their needs aside to help you get what you want. The challenge with Martyrs is that their focus is on getting sympathy and attention and not on accomplishing professional or family objectives.

The Surrender style is not useful when you want different viewpoints and solutions.

Dominate

Motto — *My way or the highway*

The Dominate style demonstrates a high level of interest in accomplishing one's own goals, and little, if any, interest in helping other people with theirs. The two types of Dominate behaviors are that of the **Terminator** and that of the **Controller.** Both types think they are always right and are condescending to others. Control is paramount for both of these types, but one may be more difficult to detect.

Terminators are intimidating, overbearing, and tyrannical. They have a "scorched earth" approach to communications. Terminators lack patience, are aggressive, demand attention, and frequently interrupt others. They are quite comfortable with the concept of collateral damage (as long as they are not the collateral). Terminators are easy to spot, and you know where they stand.

Controllers are manipulative, insidious, and oppressive. They work behind the scenes to control outcomes in their favor at the expense of others. Their machinations may be difficult to discern, with makes it difficult to identify and deal with them in a forthright manner.

The Dominate style is not recommended for building trust and deepening relationships.

Synergize

Motto — *The whole is greater than the sum of the parts*

The Synergize style demonstrates a high level of interest in accomplishing one's own goals and those of other people. Synergize behavior is that of the **Champion.** The main communication objective is **Constructive Candor.**

> "...each opens himself to the other person, truly accepts his point of view as worthy of consideration... so that they can agree with each other on a subject"
> Hans-Georg Gadamer

Constructive Candor facilitates the open exchange of information to enhance partnering, cooperating, networking, linking, sharing, interconnecting, and relationship building. **Champions** are good listeners and negotiators, and are willing to share information. They have good inquiry skills, are team oriented, and inclusive. Champions are patient and invest the time and energy to do it right the first time, by ensuring they consider various. They cooperate with others to resolve issues and develop solutions. Constructive Candor is explained more fully in the next chapter (Share and Understand).

Of the four styles, Synergize is recommended as the most effective approach for situations in which there is a need to build trust, deepen relationships, keep people on the same page, and to accomplish organizational or family goals.

The remainder of the manual provides concepts, principles, and tools to achieve and maintain a Synergize communication style, even under duress.

Which CUF Style behaviors do you exhibit, and in which situations?

Styles & Behaviors	Situations
Avoid	
Hider	_____
	_____
	_____
Dismisser	_____
	_____
	_____
Surrender	
Appeaser	_____
	_____
	_____
Martyr	_____
	_____
	_____
Dominate	
Terminator	_____
	_____
Controller	_____
	_____
	_____
Synergize	
Champion	_____
	_____
	_____
	_____
	_____

Select, from the list you just completed, one or two situations in which you did not use the most effective style and behaviors to get the results you were seeking.

Identify the situation and which style and behavior would have been more effective.

_____

_____

_____

_____

_____

What might the results have been if you used the style and behavior you identified above?

_____

_____

_____

_____

_____

_____

_____

_____

_____

_____

_____

_____

_____

_____

_____

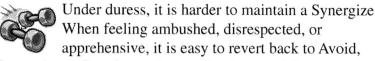 Under duress, it is harder to maintain a Synergize When feeling ambushed, disrespected, or apprehensive, it is easy to revert back to Avoid, Surrender, or Dominate. Preparation is one of the keys to having a productive conversation. Prepare yourself in advance to deal with counterproductive styles by deciding how you will behave and what you will say in tough situations.

From the point of view of the Synergize style, build a Conflict Toolkit containing strategies and key phrases to help you deal with the Avoid, Surrender, and Dominate styles. After you complete the exercise, refer to the Conflict Toolkit in the Appendix for some suggested strategies and phrases.

For example, for the Avoid style you might include:
- Strategy — Use open-ended questions
- Key Phrase — *Your contribution is valuable...*

Conflict Toolkit
Page 1

Avoid
Strategies

_____

_____

_____

_____

_____

_____

Key Phrases

_____

_____

_____

_____

_____

_____

Conflict Toolkit
Page 2

Surrender
Strategies

_____
_____
_____
_____
_____
_____

Key Phrases

_____
_____
_____
_____
_____

Dominate
Strategies

_____
_____
_____
_____

Key Phrases

_____
_____
_____
_____
_____

CUF Styles
Hot Buttons & Alarms

Based on the CUF Style information explored in this chapter, list any additional hot buttons or alarms that have surfaced.

Hot buttons are words, issues, attitudes, or situations that cause an immediate negative reaction.

_____

_____

_____

_____

_____

_____

_____

Alarms are the cues from your body that you are reacting negatively to something. If you have identified any additional alarms that warn you that a hot button has been pushed, list them here. Some examples are: heavy breathing, shallow breathing, flushing, blinking, staring, chest tightening, pacing, pounding something, pushing up on your toes.

_____

_____

_____

_____

_____

_____

_____

_____

* The Hot Button & Alarms lists at the end of Chapters 2, 3, 4, and 5 will be consolidated in Chapter 7 (*Hot Buttons & Alarms*)

CUF Commitment #2

In the heat of a high intensity conversation, I Choose to use the most effective communication style, even if it takes a lot of effort to do so.

☐ I commit

Signature   Date

_____   _____

Chapter 4
Share & Understand

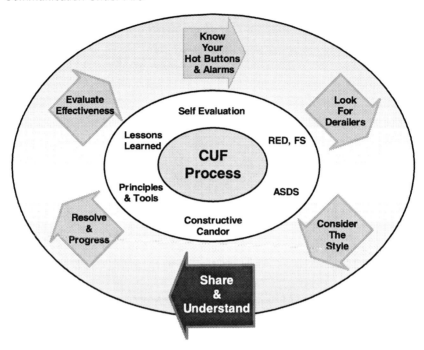

The last chapter, CUF Styles, underscored the barriers people create when not striving for open, two-way communication. It also addressed the recommended style, Synergize, as the way to achieve and maintain Constructive Candor. This chapter continues the discussion of Constructive Candor.

Constructive Candor

We have a powerful need to communicate and interact with others.

Alder, Rosenfeld, and Towne discuss an isolation experiment in which "subjects were paid to remain alone in a locked room. Of the five subjects, one lasted for eight days. Three held out for two days, one commenting, 'Never again.' The fifth subject lasted only two hours..." (1986).

Some of you are thinking, "Take me to that experiment. I'd love a little solitude". That may be true, but each of us has a limit to the amount of solitude we consider satisfying. Beyond that limit, it becomes unpleasant and we need to communicate with another person.

The deep-seated need to communicate has been with us since birth and will last throughout our lives. Our effectiveness in communicating impacts our quality of life.

"To live, then, is to communicate. To communicate effectively is to enjoy life more fully."
Hybels and Weaver (1998)

Constructive Candor enables effective communication. It is defined as *the open exchange of information with the intent of surfacing experiences and expanding understanding.*

Exploring "complex difficult issues from many points of view" (Senge, 2006), requires keeping your mind open to receive new information and look at old information in new ways. Even if you believe you have all the answers, you may not have all the best answers. Listening to others' answers and sharing your own perspectives can be of great benefit in resolving issues and developing solutions. Be willing to expand beyond your understanding and hold the belief that others have valuable insights to share and that they deserve the benefit of hearing your viewpoint.

Use the Synergize style to achieve Constructive Candor. It enables maintaining open lines of communication with others, while addressing difficult issues. In Constructive Candor you observe and regulate your own thinking and behavior. You stay attuned to whether you are using the Synergize style to stay in Constructive Candor or you have shifted to one of the less effective styles. If you move out of Constructive Candor, then consciously decide to make the necessary adjustments to get back on track.

You must play a dual role — as a participant in the conversation, and as an observer or coach. As observer or coach you can decide to self-correct and guide yourself back into Constructive Candor. One of the best ways to accomplish this is to admit your error, correct it, and do not repeat it. For example, "The last statement I made was not helpful and I apologize. Please allow me to correct my error. What I meant to say was…"

Not repeating the behavior is very important. If you keep apologizing and repeating the unacceptable behavior, it can exacerbate the situation. If someone accepts your apology then trusts you to not repeat the behavior they can feel betrayed when you continue to do it. Now you have two problems: betrayal and frustration with the unacceptable behavior itself.

To avoid this situation ask the other person to give feedback when you slip and when you succeed. Ask them to identify opportunities and make suggestions for improvement.

Constructive Candor focuses on how to communicate others so that information is shared, buy-in is achieved, and results are attained.

The next chapter, *Resolve and Progress*, addresses the principles and tools of Constructive Candor.

Share & Understand
Hot Buttons & Alarms

Based on the Constructive Candor information explored in this chapter, list any additional hot buttons or alarms that have surfaced.

Hot buttons are words, issues, attitudes, or situations that cause an immediate negative reaction.

_____

_____

_____

_____

_____

_____

Alarms are the cues from your body that you are reacting negatively to something. If you have identified any additional alarms that warn you that a hot button has been pushed, list them here. Some examples are: heavy breathing, shallow breathing, flushing, blinking, staring, chest tightening, pacing, pounding something, pushing up on your toes.

_____

_____

_____

_____

_____

_____

_____

_____

_____

* The Hot Button & Alarms lists at the end of Chapters 2, 3, 4, and 5 will be consolidated in Chapter 7 (*Hot Buttons & Alarms*)

CUF Commitment #3

I will notice whether I am in Constructive Candor. If I am not, I will use the Synergize style to get on track.

☐ I commit

Signature   Date

_____   _____

Chapter 5
Resolve & Progress

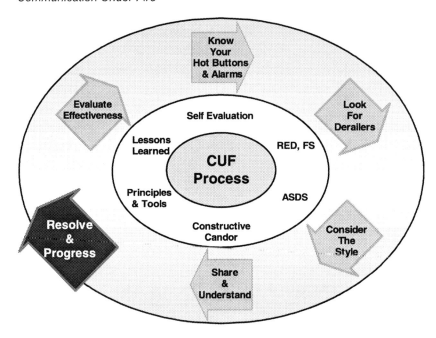

Staying in Constructive Candor while engaged in a CUF conversation requires discipline and skill. The principles and tools in this chapter provide specific guidance on how to stay on track.

Principles & Tools

The principles and tools address the mindset, attitude, resolve, and self control required to maintain Constructive Candor. They also give you a template for what to say, and how to say it. They help you create the best conditions for success. When a conversation starts heating up you have the skills to repair mistakes and misconceptions and to allow space for cooler and clearer minds to engage.

The principles and tools of Constructive Candor facilitate the behavior and mindset of the Synergize style.

PRIDE Principles

Each of the PRIDE principles addresses a different aspect of the conversational environment. If any one area is neglected, the conversation may degrade.

Purpose .... Have a shared purpose
Respect .... Treat others in a respectful manner
Inclusion .... Include the opinions of others
Determination .... Invest the time to make it right
Emotion .... Check the emotions that drive counter-
                         productive behavior

Let's explore each principle beginning with Purpose.

Principle 1 - Purpose

Shared purpose is the platform upon which the conversation builds and is the first thing that should happen. The participants should agree on the reason for the dialogue, and what is to be accomplished. This shared understanding serves as a directional beacon to steer the conversation to a successful outcome.

Once agreed upon, every aspect of the discussion should support the purpose. A shared understanding of why and how the conversation should occur provides the framework for keeping the conversation focused. Throughout the discussion, it may be necessary to steer the conversation back to the purpose with phrases such as:

- "As we agreed, the purpose of this discussion is 'X'. To accomplish our objectives in the allotted time we should maintain our focus on this topic".
- "The information you're sharing is interesting, and it may be better suited for another time. Right now, let's stay focused on 'X'.

- "It's always helpful to have an historical perspective. Let's table your comments until we get to the 'potential obstacles' section of the discussion."

Hidden agendas can stall conversations create frustration, because they run counter to the primary objective. Typically people use Hider, Controller, or Appeaser behavior to mask hidden agendas. Investing time to establish a shared purpose increases the opportunity to surface hidden agendas, and structuring an effective conversation.

Recognize that shared purpose does not mean shared strategy. You may share the purpose of the discussion, and have very different views of how to accomplish the stated objectives. Once the discussion moves to strategies and solutions the participants can lose sight of their shared purpose and discussions can intensify. When that happens restate the purpose as a reminder of your mutual intent, then acknowledge different solutions as possible approaches to dealing with the situation. Only delve into solutions after the purpose is clearly shared by all, otherwise you will not be able to leverage the purpose and focus the discussion.

The key points of agreement regarding the issue, situation, or problem being discussed:
- Topic being discussed
- Objective of the discussion – such as:
    o Define and articulate the problem
    o Resolve the issue
- Outcome or expected deliverables – such as:
    o Increased awareness
    o Solution outline
    o Action plan
- Structure of the conversation – such as:
    o Get input by asking key questions about the situation
    o Share perspectives
    o Discuss a plan of action

o   Identify potential obstacles to moving forward
o   Brainstorm strategies to overcome the obstacles
o   Implement the plan

Principle 2 - Respect

Constructive Candor requires the partners in the conversation to have a mutual regard for one another. This means viewing the other person as equal in some way and being committed to demonstrating fair-mindedness and consideration.

Through the ages, philosophers have studied and written about respect, with particular focus on respect for self and others. It is a central theme in discussions of politics, ethics, equality, diversity, inclusion, motivation, development, and justice. Some philosophers consider respect to be at the core of our morality and human interactions.

The 18th century philosopher, Immanuel Kant, was the first western philosopher to position respect for people, including oneself, as the centerpiece of morality. He believed that "personhood" itself deserves respect, just on that basis. His work has profoundly impacted western civilization.

Respect is derived from the "Latin repsectus - act of looking back, regard, consideration" (Merriam-Webster, 2006). The manner in which Person A perceives Person B influences how Person A treats Person B. In turn, Person B responds to the way Person A treats them. Do you respond the same way to someone who listens to you and looks interested in what you are saying, as you do to someone who acts indifferent, bored, or dismissive towards you? Of course not. Even if you are not rude to the dismissive person, you might not go out of your way to volunteer helpful information, and you might even avoid them in the future.

We each define respect differently. Each of us has a set of behaviors, actions, and attitudes associated with respect. Others' behavior conveys the level of respect they have, and we respond accordingly. For example, in some cultures it is considered a show of respect to eat everything that is placed before you, lest you offend the host. It would be insulting for you to say, "No thank you, I'm not hungry."

Given the ambiguity of respect, it behooves you to watch for indications that others are offended by what you have done or said. If you see or sense an offense has occurred, then correct the situation before proceeding with the conversation, as follows:

> "From your reaction, it seems the last statement I made was offensive and I apologize. *I did not mean to disrespect or insult you. What I meant to say was...*"

Explicitly stating what you do NOT intend is powerful and effective. It is interesting to observe that even people who have not studied communication theory or the psychology of human interaction, frequently use "not intend" statements. This is particularly true in high stakes situations where it is critical to convey your good intentions as soon as possible. The next time you see a movie or television show about the gangland subculture, you will probably hear someone who is in a vulnerable position preface his statement to a more powerful and dangerous person, with, "I don't mean any disrespect..."

In deciding on the value of repairing perceptions of disrespect, put yourself in the other person's shoes by asking yourself whether you feel like engaging in Constructive Candor when you feel you have been "dissed" — disrespected, discredited, dishonored, or disavowed. If the answer is "no", then realize conversations cannot constructively progress until all involved feel respected.

Principle 3 - Inclusion

Inclusion is about valuing the unique qualities and perspectives that others bring to the conversation. Constructive Candor's "open exchange of information" is a two-way process. Inclusion focuses on listening and asking questions.

"Many attempts to communicate are nullified by saying too much"
Robert Greenleaf (1977)

Listening helps us receive the information we need, and get buy-in from people from whom we need support. It helps build trust because others appreciate being listened to. It makes them feel interesting and respected.

There are three primary listening modes.

- **Combative Listeners** are interested in promoting a personal agenda. They listen for flaws, weak points, and pauses to attack or retake the floor. While pretending to pay attention, they formulate rebuttals and develop searing responses leaving others feeling defeated and humiliated. This listening approach is based on the concept of 'I win – you lose'!

  To avoid combative listening, take a deep breath and stop thinking about yourself. Focus on the words and meaning of others and let them finish speaking. Pause and think before responding, consider whether your view has changed and respond respectfully.

- **Passive Listeners** are sincerely interested in what is being said. They make assumptions about what they hear with no verification. Others interpret passive listening as unengaged and indifferent.

67

Passive listeners should be more engaged and interested and, at the end of the conversation, summarize what you heard. Practice active listening, which we discuss next.

- **Active Listeners** are sincerely interested in what others are saying: the words, the context, and thoughts and feelings. They summarize and rephrase to assure understanding before speaking. They make eye contact and use engaging body language to signal interest and attention. They also share observations about appropriately. For example, "You seem to be troubled," or "I can see you are quite excited". Active listening, the most useful and powerful listening skill, is based on the concept of 'I win – you win!'

  If active listening, even in CUF conversations, is your primary mode, then congratulations are in order. Combative and Passive Listeners should strive to become Active Listeners.

Being interested in and willing to listen to others sets the stage for you to use your listening skills. Listening requires the other person to share information. In situations in which the other person has difficulty saying what is on their mind, we may have to win confidence, or engage the other person by asking questions that help surface information. Questions are used to:
- Obtain information
- Arouse interest
- Diagnose a situation
- Ascertain attitudes, feelings and opinions
- Encourage critical thought
- Maintain another's attention.

The best way to encourage someone to talk is by asking open-ended questions, which cannot be answered with at "yes" or "no." These questions are broad and encourage another to talk longer and more deeply. For example, you would say, "What steps were taken to implement this policy?" rather than, "Was the policy implemented."

It is important to ask questions without interrogating. An interrogation feels intrusive and may cause others to become defensive and shut down. The questions should be an invitation to share thoughts and experiences. Open-ended questions and relaxed body language help invite disclosure.

Principle 4 - Determination

In our fast-paced world, the velocity with which we propel from one thing to the next can lead to impatience. At times we neglect to slow down long enough to get critical information that ultimately precludes having to backtrack.

Using the Synergize style to stay in Constructive Candor positively impacts a conversation. Others using the Avoid, Surrender, or Dominate style may not immediately respond to your constructive approach. However, stick with it and remember:

- Stay on track
- Encourage others to elevate their behavior

Others will notice you are consistently staying in Constructive Candor, even when they are not participating. You may be tested but keep your focus. Others' behavior may escalate by as they engage in more avoidance, surrendering more quickly and frequently, or becoming more dominating. Anticipating unproductive will eliminate surprises and help you remain focused. The power of role-modeling the Synergize style to influence others happens when people observe that, in CUF conversations with them and others, you:

- Seem interested and enthusiastic, yet emotionally calm
- Address unacceptable behavior in a forthright manner
- Clarify meaning and intent
- Contribute helpful information

•   Discuss the undiscussable in safe and constructive ways

Over time, even the most recalcitrant person may learn to develop trust and modify his/her behavior in conversations, as we will see in Principle 5 with the case of Tom, the executive.

Principle 5 - Emotion

Runaway emotions can cause us to shift out of the Synergize style. When an emotion "comes out of nowhere," it can instantly cause a behavior change and we may unconsciously display counterproductive behavior.

The benefits of consistent use of Constructive Candor are most apparent when we are in CUF conversations. With practice, the Synergize style becomes second nature, even under stress. Negative emotions release toxic chemicals in our bodies and brains, challenging rational thought. With just a little effort, good habits can override our baser instincts. The more we use the principles and tools of Constructive Candor, the easier it is to recall and use them under pressure.

Tom, an executive in a Fortune 100 company, is intelligent, creative, and quick; however, he is impatient and has a swift temper. He needed to strengthen his leadership skills and role-model the behavior he expected from the managers and employees in his business unit. Everyone knew he would wait about three seconds before cutting you off by: (1) finishing your thought before you could; (2) switching to a new subject; or (3) e-mailing on his computer or handheld PDA. He did this even when he initiated the conversation.

With the help of feedback, he realized his behavior was an obstacle to creating the type of organization that could accomplish their ambitious goals, and he resolved to improve. Working together, Tom and I paid special attention to respect, listening, and delegation. He had a difficult time understanding and applying the concepts and became anxious when he could not interrupt or multi-task during conversations. He felt that listening was a time consuming waste of energy. According to Tom, his anxiety level drove him to act on his negative impulses.

With practice, Tom was able to quiet his emotions and consistently engage in Constructive Candor. To his credit, he stuck with the program we established, completely changed his behavior, and was elated with the results. His staff is pleased with the new and improved Tom. The managers who report to him are able to assume more responsibility because Tom provides developmental opportunities, information and guidance, and he is listening to their perspectives. Six months later he called to say, "I expected to change my behavior so I could develop my organization, but I got the added bonus of feeling happier, calmer, and personally being more productive."

Tools

The Communication Under Fire™ tools are clear, simple, and powerful and can be quickly integrated into your life. They are shortcuts that prescribe what to say, do, and think in CUF conversations. Memorizing and practicing these tools prepares you for pressure situations. Use them to stay in Constructive Candor and keep the conversation productive. These are the tools that will help you be more effective:

- RE-Tool
- ARM
- But-Out
- Fact

RE-Tool
RE-Tool allows you to stop and consider your actions, check for understanding and agreement, and add background information to enhance comprehension.

- **REcede** – Think before speaking. Decide on the best approach to achieve your outcome, then speak.
- **REplay** – Rephrase what the other person said to assure understanding.
- **REplenish** – Clarify your own point of view to avoid and resolve misunderstandings.

ARM

When someone confronts or argues with you, calmly and firmly assert yourself, instead of Avoiding, Surrendering, or Dominating. Using the Synergize style:

- Acknowledge what is being said by replaying what you heard and recognizing the other person's intensity and emotion.
- Restate and clarify your position, adding additional supporting data if necessary
- Move the conversation forward by stating what you see as the next steps.

For example:
"I understand why you need that information. However, I'm not able to provide it today because I'm leaving for an all-day regional review meeting. I'd be happy to give you the report I prepared last week, and if you'd like, I'll also give you the new raw data so that you can compile the latest results".

But-Out

Eliminate the word "but" from the discussion. It discounts or diminishes the information that preceded it. "But" can shut down a smoothly flowing conversation, or amplify a CUF one.

We have all said something like, "I understand what you are saying, **but…**" Instead of discounting what was just said, build on it, or just take the discussion in a new direction. Mention the aspects with which you agree, then say, "**…and** I have also found…" Substituting "and" for "but" indicates that you are building on at least some of what was said. If you completely disagree with what the other person said, use the ARM tool, if appropriate, and simply state your position.

FACT

Chapter 2 discussed the Left-Hand Column as containing unresolved issues or emotions. Now let us talk about how to clear them out.

FACT is a simple and powerful way to clear your Left-Hand Column of negative emotions. It helps you convey what you observed, how you interpreted it, and how it made you feel, and then ask for the other person's perspective.

- **F**acts first – Begin by stating your observations without any embellishment or interpretation of meaning.
  "Sarah, when you entered the room I smiled and waved and you did not respond."
- **A**ssumptions – Clearly identify this as your interpretation and not fact.
  "I assumed you didn't want to connect with me."
- **C**onclusions – Tell how it made you feel and what you concluded as a result.
  "I figured you were distancing yourself from me and that I could no longer depend on your support."
- **T**est your scenario – Ask the other person whether your assumptions and conclusions are correct.
  "Is that true, is that really what's going on?"

Engage / Disengage

Staying engaged in Constructive Candor requires focus, commitment, and skills. Because it is the right thing to do, we overcome our urges to Avoid, Surrender, or Dominate and shift into Synergize to work toward a productive outcome.

However, there are times when your best approach is to disengage. This is likely if there is little mutual value in the relationship, the objective, or in resolving the issue. Disengage respectfully, with no display of negative emotions.

In CUF conversations:

Which of the PRIDE* principles are easy for you to follow? Why?

_____

_____

_____

_____

_____

Which of the PRIDE principles are difficult for you to follow? Why?

_____

_____

_____

_____

_____

_____

How will you overcome your difficulties in following the PRIDE principles?

_____

_____

_____

_____

_____

_____

_____

_____

_____

* PRIDE – Purpose, Respect, Inclusion, Determination, Emotion

Make copies of this PRIDE checklist and use it when preparing for CUF conversations. Write down your strategies for adhering to each principle.

Pride Checklist

☐ Purpose................Have a shared purpose

_____

_____

_____

☐ Respect.................Treat others in a respectful manner

_____

_____

_____

☐ Inclusion ....Include the perspective of others

_____

_____

_____

☐ Determination.........Invest the time to make it right

_____

_____

_____

☐ Emotion.................Check emotions that drive counter-productive behavior

_____

_____

_____

_____

You must use the tools if you want them to work for you. These activities will help you incorporate them into your conversational toolkit.

Think of a recent conversation that went poorly, or didn't happen at all. How do you think the conversation would have been improved if you had used RE-Tool to stop and consider your actions, check for understanding and agreement, and add background information to enhance comprehension?

_____

_____

_____

_____

_____

_____

Recall a situation in which you were engaged in an argument. Did you handle it effectively? How would the ARM tool have moved the discussion forward? Would you have felt calmer and in control? Practice ARM in front of a mirror. Check your eyes to ensure they look calm and confident. How do you feel using ARM? Keep practicing it until it feels comfortable.

_____

_____

_____

_____

_____

For one week, count the number of times you use 'but' to discount what someone just said. Record the number below. Continue to do it until the number is zero.

_____

_____

_____

_____

If FACT is so easy, why not you use it every time it is needed?

Will it be easy for you to use FACT every time you feel angry, frustrated, slighted, misunderstood, or disrespected – and need to clear the air?

_____

_____

_____

_____

If no, what are your obstacles to using it?

_____

_____

_____

_____

_____

_____

_____

_____

_____

How can you overcome the obstacles you listed above?

_____

_____

_____

_____

_____

_____

Resolve & Progress
Hot Buttons & Alarms

Based on the Principles & Tools information explored in this chapter, list any **additional** hot buttons or alarms that have surfaced.

Hot buttons are words, issues, attitudes, or situations that cause an immediate negative reaction.

_____

_____

_____

_____

_____

_____

Alarms are the cues from your body that you are reacting negatively to something. If you have identified any additional alarms that warn you that a hot button has been pushed, list them here. Some examples are: heavy breathing, shallow breathing, flushing, blinking, staring, chest tightening, pacing, pounding something, pushing up on your toes.

_____

_____

_____

_____

_____

_____

_____

_____

* The Hot Button & Alarms lists at the end of Chapters 2, 3, 4, and 5 will be consolidated in Chapter 7 (*Hot Buttons & Alarms*)

CUF Commitment #4

I will practice using the PRIDE checklist to ensure I am following all of the Constructive Candor principles.

I will use RE-Tool and ARM to move conversations forward.

I will 'But-Out' and not discount what the other person said prior to sharing my perspective.

I will use FACT to clear out my Left-Hand Column.

☐ I commit

Signature   Date

_____   _____

Chapter 6
Evaluate Effectiveness

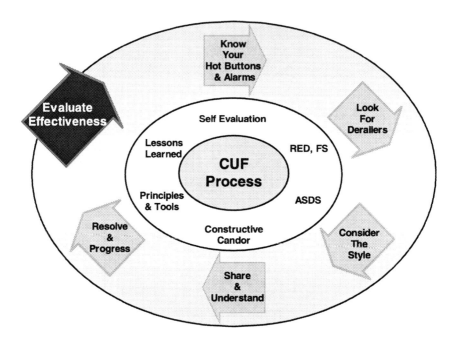

Each of us has a different starting point or baseline, but with commitment and attention we can all end up at the same place — Constructive Candor mastery. This chapter discusses how to track your progress in using the CUF tools to improve effectiveness.

After CUF conversations, spend time debriefing to evaluate your level of success. Write down what went well and what needs to be improved. Identify what you will do to improve the tone and direction of the conversation. Pinpoint any counterproductive behaviors you exhibited, why you engaged in those behaviors, and what you can do to avoid falling into that trap again.

Assessment is critical to your continued success because it helps you stay focused on the objective. Focus and commitment are necessary to anchor the new behavior so that it becomes your default go-to position. The saying "old habits die hard" succinctly articulates the neurological challenges in changing our behavior. Habits help us navigate our day by eliminating the need to rethink each familiar step, such as taking a shower or driving to work. Bad habits can have an insidious and powerful hold on us. They can recede and "play possum" for a while, then suddenly resurface taking hold of both mind and behavior.

Ann Graybiel, professor of Neuroscience in MIT's Department of Brain and Cognitive Sciences, found that neural activity patterns "change when habits are formed, change again when habits are broken, and then re-emerge when something rekindles an extinguished habit." According to Ann, "We knew that neurons can change their firing patterns when habits are learned, but it is startling to find that these patterns reverse when the habit is lost, only to recur again as soon as something kicks off the habit again" (Delude, 2005).

The implication for learning new communication behaviors is that certain situations, events, or people can trigger old patterns that flip you back into Avoid, Surrender, or Dominate styles. Assessing effectiveness helps to ascertain your progress. It also surfaces backsliding so that you can catch yourself early and recommit to staying in Constructive Candor.

The assessment tool that follows helps evaluate your increasing effectiveness. The first time you take it you establish a baseline against which to measure future progress. Use this assessment every month until you reach your desired level. Then use it several times a year to see how you are maintaining your new level of mastery.

CUF Assessment

Mark the column that indicates the degree to which your behavior matches the following statements.

	Almost Always				Almost Never	Not Apply
	5	4	3	2	1	0

1. I use the Synergize style to stay in Constructive Candor when:
   Faced with risky situations
   Negative emotions bubble up
   I have differences that seem to 'get in the way'

2. When I perceive a negative intent behind what someone says or does, I challenge my assumptions and conclusions.

3. List the undiscussables interfering in your work and personal life, then respond to the following statement about each undiscussable.
   "I constructively address this undiscussable."

   _____
   _____
   _____
   _____

4. I use the FACT tool to clear my Left-Hand Column.

5. I use RE-Tool to pause, consider my actions and contribute helpful information.

6. I use ARM to respectfully disagree and move the the conversation forward.

7. I have eliminated the word 'but' from my vocabulary.

Questions 8-10 refer to situations in which you have typically used the Avoid, Surrender, or Dominate style.

8. Respond to the following statements if you have used the Avoid style:
   I share my perspective with others
   I am willing to have a constructive conversation
   I respect myself and the other person

9. Respond to the following statements if you have used the Surrender style:
   I am flexible, but I don't 'rollover'
   I focus on accomplishing my objectives
   I respect myself

10. Respond to the following statements if you have used the Dominate style:
    I give the other person a chance to talk
    I listen while the other person is talking
    I respect the other person

11. Conversations that used to yield poor results are now:
    Easier to have
    Yield better results

Scoring

* Add each column, then add column totals to compute the grand total   = _____

* Divide the grand total by 24 to compute your score   [   ]

Score Key	5 = Very Effective; 4 = Effective; 3 = Somewhat Effective; 2 = Ineffective 1 = Very Ineffective

Chapter 7
Hot Buttons & Alarms

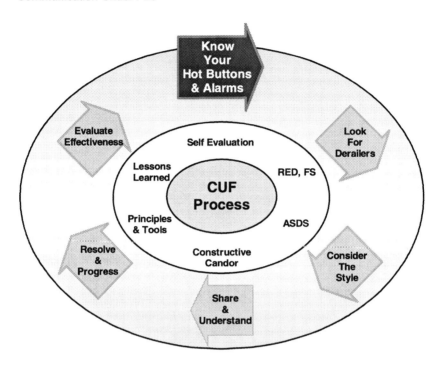

Adopting new communication behaviors requires self-awareness and self-management. Throughout this manual you have been recording your Hot Buttons and Alarms. This chapter focuses on consolidating that information and putting it to good use.

Knowing these triggers gives you the power to overcome and replace old behaviors with new more effective ones. As we discussed in the last chapter, Evaluate Effectiveness, "old habits die hard." If you know ahead of time which situations, styles, or people cause you to slip into old patterns, you can prepare yourself with strategies and tactics to avoid the siren call of the triggers.

Know Your Hot Buttons

The goal is for you to be aware of the negative emotions evoked by your hot buttons and alarms, and choose to override their pull toward inappropriate behavior, and to substitute rational productive behavior. When you interact with button-pushing people or situations you can feel anxious, demoralized, unmotivated, powerless, and angry. These emotions revive the old patterns that cause you to shut down, lash out, assume the worst, and blame others. According to Goleman (2005), this experience is called "neural hijacking." Your emotional brain perceives a threat, declares an emergency situation, and springs into action executing old familiar behavior patterns. It happens so quickly that often you are responding before your cognitive or thinking brain is fully aware of what is happening.

Your Hot Buttons and Alarms list should be updated when circumstances change. After you have diffused a hot button and find that it no longer triggers a negative reaction, then retire it from the list. If it re-emerges, then add it back. When new situations or circumstances create fresh hot buttons, include them in your list.

You may be tempted to remove "active" hot buttons that you are effectively handling. Keep them on the list. It is great that you are not being blindsided by them. But since they are having an emotional impact, they could take control if you have a really bad day or are fatigued. Keeping them on the list reminds you to maintain your vigilance.

Consolidate the Hot Buttons and Alarms you recorded at the end of Chapters 2 – 5. What will you do differently in the future? What strategies and tools will you use? Refer to Conflict Toolkit (Chapter 3 and Appendix), and Principles & Tools (Chapter 5). Make copies of your consolidated list and carry it with you until you consistently respond effectively in CUF situations.

Hot Buttons & Alarms

Hot Button / Alarm

_____

_____

What will you do differently to stay in Constructive Candor?

_____

_____

_____

Hot Button / Alarm

_____

_____

What will you do differently to stay in Constructive Candor?

_____

_____

_____

Hot Button / Alarm

_____

_____

What will you do differently to stay in Constructive Candor?

_____

_____

_____

_____

Hot Buttons & Alarms

Hot Button / Alarm

_____

_____

What will you do differently to stay in Constructive Candor?

_____

_____

_____

_____

Hot Button / Alarm

_____

_____

What will you do differently to stay in Constructive Candor?

_____

_____

_____

_____

Hot Button / Alarm

_____

_____

What will you do differently to stay in Constructive Candor?

_____

_____

_____

_____

Chapter 8

Application to Your Situation

Refer to the notes you made on the **organization** activity sheet in the Impact of Communication section of Chapter 1 *(Overview)*, and on the activity sheets in the Undiscussables section of Chapter 2 *(Dimensions & Derailers)*. Answer the following question. How will I apply the Communication Under Fire™ concepts, principles, and tools, to positively impact my **team, group, or organization?**

Refer to the notes you made on the **personal life** activity sheet in the Impact of Communication section of Chapter 1 (*Overview*). Answer the following question. How will I apply the Communication Under Fire™ concepts, principles, and tools, to positively impact my **personal life?**

In summary, the Communication Under Fire™ system:
- Articulates key concepts that explain why communication is difficult in CUF situations
- Provides a model to show you what to do to improve effectiveness in every situation
- Delivers simple and powerful tools that illustrate how to do it right

The CUF Process wheel below summarizes the key elements of the system. Use it as a tool to direct your actions toward effective communications. Using the techniques described in the Communication Under Fire™ system, you will reap the rewards of effective communications.

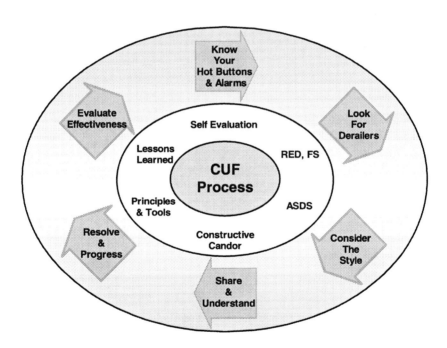

References

Adler, R.B., Rosenfeld, L.B., & Towne, N. (1986). Interplay: *The Process of Interpersonal Communication.* New York: CBS College Press.

Argyris, Chris. 1990. *Overcoming Organizational Defenses.* New York: Prentice-Hall.

Bar-On, R. & Parker, J.D.A. (Eds.) (2000). The handbook of emotional intelligence. San Francisco: Jossey-Bass.

Cherniss, C., & Goleman, D. (2001). *The Emotionally Intelligent Workplace.* San Francisco: Jossey-Bass.

Delude, C.M. (2005). *Brain researchers explain why old habits die hard.* MIT News Office. Available: http://web.mit.edu/ newsoffice/2005/habit.html

Gadamer, H-G. (1979) *Truth and Method.* London: Sheed and Ward.

Gallagher, Sean (2001). "Bringing Clarity to Business Goals." Baseline Project Management Center. December 10, 2001. Available: http://www.baselinemag.com/article2/ 0,1397,819064,00.asp

Goleman, D. (2005). *Emotional Intelligence.* New York: Bantam.

Greenleaf, R. (2002). *Servant Leadership.* New Jersey: Paulist Press.

Hargie, O., & Dickson, D. ((2004). *Skilled Interpersonal Communication.* New York: Routledge.

Hughes, M., Patterson, L.B., & Terrell, J.B. (2005). *Emotional Intelligence in Action* San Francisco: Pfeiffer.

Hybels, S., & Weaver R. (1998). *Communicating Effectively.* New York: Harper & Row.

Merriam-Webster Unabridged Dictionary. (2006). Available: http://unabridged.merriam-webster.com.

The Public Relations Society of America (2003). "A Cost of Corporate Jargon." The Strategist. New York: Public Relations Society of America.

Senge, P.M. (1990) *The Fifth Discipline.* New York: Doubleday Currency.

Symanovich, Steve (2003). "Poor Communication Plagues Medical Profession." *Houston Business Journal,* October 17, 2003. Available: http://www.bizjournals.com/houston/ stories/2003/10/20/editorial3.html

Appendix

Conflict Toolkit

The following Conflict Toolkit contains strategies and key phrases to use in dealing with different CUF styles. Use the blank lines to add phrases and strategies you developed during the activity Chapter 3 *(Styles)*.

Conflict Toolkit

Dealing With an *Avoid* Communication Style

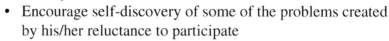

Strategies
- Create a safe and secure environment
- Use open-ended questions
- Actively listen; let the other person know you are interested
- Encourage self-discovery of some of the problems created by his/her reluctance to participate
- Keep them focused on the issue at hand

Add additional strategies:

_____

_____

_____

_____

_____

_____

Key Phrases

- I'm really interested in what you're thinking/feeling about _____.
- What do you think/feel about _____.
- Your contribution is valuable.
- When you don't say anything, I don't know how you feel or what you think/conclude.
- I need your input if we are going to resolve _____.
- Are you concerned that I will react negatively if you are honest with me?

Add additional phrases:

_____

_____

_____

_____

_____

Dealing With a *Surrender* Communication Style

Strategies

- Create a safe and secure environment
- Help them understand that you will not use their opinions against them
- Clarify how surfacing different perspectives contributes to better decision making
- Encourage self-discovery of some of the problems created by his/her approach
- Ask for solutions
- Ask what actions they think should be taken

Add additional strategies:

_____

_____

_____

_____

_____

Key Phrases

- Please describe a different way to look as this.
- What do you think/feel about _____?
- We need to factor in other viewpoints if we are going to make a good decision. Can you think of any potential opposing opinions?
- What do you think people who are seeing things the way we see them are thinking?
- How will that impact you / us / organization?
- Help me understand _____.
- Who would you implement _____?

Add additional phrases:

_____

_____

_____

_____

Dealing With a *Dominate* Communication Style

Strategies

- If you believe you are in physical danger, vacate the scene immediately, otherwise...
- Check yourself
    - o Are you baiting the other person, or fanning the flames of aggression
    - o Are you overreacting to the other person?
- Separate the person from the behavior
    - o Address the specific behavior
    - o Don't conclude the person is bad or wrong
    - o Do you know of any exacerbating factors amplifying the person's aggression, e.g., work or family pressures
- Assert yourself by expressing your point of view without hostility, sarcasm, or rancor
- Discuss the ineffectiveness of the interchange, and seek agreement to mutually work on strengthening the relationship and deepening understanding
- Encourage self-discovery of some of the problems created by his/her approach

Add additional strategies:

_____

_____

_____

_____

_____

Key Phrases

- When you speak in that manner, it makes me think that _____.
- Will you work with me to resolve _____.
- That's an interesting perspective.
- Let me build on what you said, and share with you how I see things a little differently.

- You've made me curious, would you share with me the data that lead you to that conclusion?

Add additional phrases:

_____

_____

_____

_____

_____

CPSIA information can be obtained at www.ICGtesting.com
Printed in the USA
BVOW070006130412

287574BV00002B/6/A